Books by Bill Adler

THE KENNEDY WIT
THE CHURCHILL WIT
THE STEVENSON WIT
THE JOHNSON HUMOR
KIDS LETTERS TO PRESIDENT KENNEDY
DEAR PRESIDENT JOHNSON
LOVE LETTERS TO THE METS
LOVE LETTERS TO THE BEATLES
LETTERS FROM CAMP
BOYS ARE VERY FUNNY PEOPLE

Dear

Senator

Kennedy

Edited by Bill Adler

DODD, MEAD & COMPANY, New York

Photographs courtesy Wide World Photos, United Press International,
PIX (Tom Blau, Carl L. Howard).

These letters were selected from the thousands of letters that Robert Kennedy has received since the assassination of his brother, President Kennedy, and his election to the United States Senate.

They express the views and sentiments of millions of Americans from all walks of life and from all fifty states. Some of these letters—especially from youngsters are touched with humor. Some are very personal—others serious and hopeful.

Few Americans have been the object of such outpouring of emotion.

I am grateful to Senator Kennedy's fine staff for their assistance in the selection of these letters.

I believe they tell more than the words of a hundred historians how we all feel—young and old—about that great tragedy in November 1963, and of the man—Robert F. Kennedy—who has dedicated himself to carry on the work his brother began.

Bill Adler
New York City

Dear Senator Robert Kennedy,

I like you very much but why does your hair always look so mussed?

You are a United States Senator now and if you don't mind my saying so, as a United States Senator you should brush your hair at least twice a day.

Respectfully yours,
Mrs. Mimi S
Hollywood, California

Dear Senator Kennedy,

If you will send me a picture of you when you were a kid, I will send you a picture of me when I was a kid.

I am 9.

Your friend,
Alvin W
Lawrence, Massachusetts

Dear Senator Kennedy,

Maybe this isn't my place to say so but as a mother I think you are too thin.

A man who leads such an active busy life as you needs his strength.

My husband and my two sons are healthy strong men because I give them plenty of meat and potatoes.

I will be honored to send you some recipes I have for dishes like lasagna that will help you put on some weight.

Sincerely,
Mrs. Robin M
Fall River, Massachusetts

Dear Senator Kennedy,

You and Soupy Sales are the best looking on TV.

Love,
Claudia P
Los Angeles, California

Dear Senator Kennedy,

Please send me all the information you have on the U.S.A.

Yours truly,
David Y
Hollywood, California

P.S. Please don't leave anything out.

Dear Mr. Senator Kennedy,

I would like to know if you have pictures of all the Kennedys in politics.

Please send them to me even if the pictures don't look too good.

Your friend,
Jenny K
New York City, New York

Dear Senator Kennedy,

What is your opinion of world war.
Is it good for anything?

Yours truly,
Jane S
Nashville, Tennessee

Dear Senator Kennedy,

May I work in your office this summer?
I could spy on the other Senators for you.

So long,
Hillard K
Philadelphia, Pennsylvania

Dear Senator Kennedy,

It must be great to have a brother with you in the U. S. Senate because now you can both share the same stationery.

> Best Wishes,
> Dick J
> Jenkintown, Pennsylvania

Dear Senator Kennedy,

I went to the library to look for a book on how to get to be Pres. of the U. S. and I couldn't find any.
Can you please send me one.

> Murray G
> New Orleans, Louisiana

Dear Senator Kennedy,

I sure heard a lot about you.
Were you famous before you were born?

> Your pal,
> Red C
> Wilmington, Delaware

Dear Senator Robert Kennedy,

You will go down in history as the Senator with the most kids.

Congratulations.

> Yours,
> Mr. Jeff K
> Columbus, Ohio

Dear Senator Kennedy,

Does the U. S. give medals for good kids.
I have been good all year and I didn't get any medals.

> Love,
> Barry J
> Chicago, Illinois

Dear Senator Kennedy,

We visited the U. S. Senate and we saw you but you didn't see us.

You were sitting on your seat and listening to the other Senators talk. You didn't say much.

Were you tired or didn't you have anything to say?

> Sincerely,
> Mrs. Molly Z
> Duluth, Minnesota

Dear Mr. Kennedy,

Last night I dreamed I was President of the United States.

Isn't that a funny dream because I'm not even old enough to vote.

> Yours,
> Barry W
> Chicago, Illinois

Dear Mr. Robert Kennedy,

I think all the Kennedys are terrific. Even Caroline and John Jr. and they haven't even done anything yet.

> Love,
> Patsy W
> Bakersfield, California

Dear Senator Kennedy,

My name is Jenny Walters and I live in Seattle, Washington.

I was wondering if you could call me up on the telephone. I certainly would have a real thrill talking to you.

> Yours,
> Jenny W
> Seattle, Washington

P. S. I promise to stop talking when the three minutes are up.

Dear Senator Kennedy,

Please let me go up in the next space ship with the astronauts.

I am 4 ft. 6 and I don't take up much room.

Dexter J
Rochester, Minnesota

Dear Senator Kennedy,

Do you think a boy who is not a good speller could be a U. S. Senator?

I would like to know before I decide what I want to be when I grow up.

Your pal,
Terry G
Fremont, Ohio

Dear Senator Kennedy,

I sure would give anything if I could have dinner at your house or lunch or breakfast.

Even a small snack in between meals would be terrific. I am a loyal Democrat.

Yours sincerely,
William W
Dover, Delaware

Dear Senator Kennedy,

Could you please pass a law so we can have dogs at 123 North St.

Our landlord is against them.

Your friend,
Richie R
New York City, New York

Dear Senator Robert Kennedy,

Will you be my valentine?

I have lots of other boy friends but if you will be my valentine I will drop them like hot cakes.

Love,
Wilma J
Springfield, Missouri

Dear Robert Kennedy,

I was only 8 years old when President Kennedy died but I will never forget him.

8 years old may be very young but I was smart enough to know that JFK was one of our greatest Presidents.

Yours truly,
Charles B
Baltimore, Maryland

Dear Senator Bobby Kennedy,

There are nine kids in your family and there are nine kids in my family.

Why don't we get your family and my family together sometime and we will have some crowd.

Yours truly,
Tillie A
Boston, Massachusetts

Dear Senator Kennedy,

Did you ever hear of James Bond?

He is the greatest. I think you should get him to work for the FBI. Then we wouldn't have any more troubles with crooks or spys.

A pal,
Edward W
Lynchburg, Virginia

Dear Senator Robert Kennedy,

Could you please tell me how I can get my son into West Point.

I think he would make a fine soldier.

I look forward to hearing from you as soon as possible. Right now my son is 8 months old.

Yours sincerely,
Jerome J
Boise, Idaho

Dear Senator Robert F Kennedy,

My name is Kevin Kennedy and I live in Chicago but I am not a relative. I wish I was.

All the kids in my class think I am a relative and boy am I popular.

I haven't told them the truth yet.

> Yours,
> Kevin K
> Chicago, Illinois

Dear Senator Kennedy,

Please investigate my teacher.
I think she is a spy.

> Your friend,
> Marcel W
> Raleigh, North Carolina

Dear Senator Kennedy,

What size shoes do you wear?
I know that sounds like a silly question but I am 12 and I hope to be a U. S. Senator from New York so I expect to step into your shoes some day.

> Yours truly,
> James A
> Bronx, New York

Dear Senator Robert Kennedy,

I am the mother of two teenage girls who are crazy about you and Ted Kennedy.

I would appreciate it very much if you could send me an autographed picture of yourself and Senator Ted Kennedy.

Frankly, I am very pleased that they have a crush on you and your brother.

Last year it was the Beatles.

Sincerely yours,
Mrs. Lawrence G
Denver, Colorado

Dear Senator Kennedy,

Do you think we will ever have a lady President?
If you do could you please tell me how it could be me.

Yours truly,
Agnes A
Hollywood, California

Dear Senator Kennedy,

It must be fun to live in Washington.

I live in Chicago. It isn't so much fun to live in Chicago because there are a lot of crooks here.

Your friend,
Richard W
Chicago, Illinois

Dear Senator Kennedy,

Please don't climb any more mountains.
We need you on the ground.

Love,
Rachel W
Lawrence, Long Island,
New York

Dear Senator Kennedy,

What will you do for the kids of the U.S.A.?
Please write your answer before the next election.

Your friend,
Irving G
Albany, New York

Dear Senator Kennedy,

Some day if you are President you will have a big problem.

You see you have 9 kids and I don't think they have room for 9 kids in the White House.

So long for now,
Duane H
New Orleans, Louisiana

Dear Senator Kennedy,

John F Kennedy gave his life for his country. He died because he fought for the dignity of man.

I think Congress should give JFK the Medal of Honor.

> Respectfully,
> Mrs. John R
> Chicago, Illinois

Dear Robert Kennedy,

When I grow up I want to be a great man like your brother President Kennedy.

I am studying everything President Kennedy ever did. I hope you don't think I'm a copycat.

> Your pal,
> Len W
> Washington, D. C.

Dear Mr. Kennedy,

You have nine kids and that is keen because now you have your own baseball team.

> Your friend,
> Noel V
> Chicago, Illinois
> Age 10

Dear Robert Kennedy,

I would have willingly given my own life to save President Kennedy. His death was the most tragic event in my lifetime.

I can still hear his words "Ask not what your country can do for you but what you can do for your country."

Now, more than ever, those words have important meaning.

I pray that you will show us the way Senator so that we can contribute to our country which gave us a great President — John F. Kennedy.

> Respectfully,
> Gloria R
> Paramount, California

Dear Mr. Kennedy,

I am glad that you are the Senator from New York because we need more help than any other place in the U. S. A.

> Your friend,
> Stan M
> New York City, New York

Dear Bobby Kennedy,

We are counting on you to keep the memory and dreams of John F. Kennedy alive for generations to come and I know that you won't let us down.

> Very truly,
> Eugene S
> Salem, Massachusetts

Dear Senator Robert Kennedy,

I sure would like to have your picture.

I never had the picture of anyone important before except the picture I got of Mickey Mantle with bubble gum.

> Your little friend,
> Alvin Z
> Oakland, California

Dear Robert Kennedy,

I will never forget how you looked when you came off the plane that brought President Kennedy back to Washington.

And I will always remember the bravery and courage of the Kennedy family at the President's funeral.

You all made it easier for us to live through the unbelievable events of November.

> Sincerely,
> Mrs. Howard M
> Washington, D. C.

Dear Robert Kennedy,

Please don't run for President until 1976 so I can vote for you.

The reason is I never voted for a Kennedy in my whole life.

> Love,
> Richard C
> Boston, Massachusetts

Dear Bobby Kennedy,

I hope you will let your younger brother Teddy run for President if he wants to even if you want to be President yourself.

I hope you will do this because nobody ever gives a kid brother a break.

I know because I am a kid brother.

> Your friend,
> Neal S
> Chicago, Illinois

Dear Senator Kennedy,

I would like to meet you. So would my mother, my father and my sister

My brother would like to meet you too but he is only 1 year old and he wouldn't even know who you are.

> Your friend,
> Patty W
> Malden, Massachusetts

Dear Mr. Kennedy,

My mother thinks you are the greatest man on earth.

Please write to her and tell her I don't have to drink three glasses of milk a day.

> Your friend,
> Albert R
> Las Cruces, New Mexico

Dear Senator Kennedy,

Next time you climb a mountain I would like to go with you.

I am ten years old and I have strong feet.

> Your fan,
> Ricardo J
> Birmingham, Alabama

Dear Senator Kennedy,

You don't know me but I have been a Kennedy fan all my life.

I am 9 and some day I hope to be a U. S. Senator like you and your brother, Ted.

My name isn't Kennedy. It is O'Brien. But I hope to make the name of O'Brien as famous as Kennedy in the near future.

> Thank you,
> Jimmy O
> Chicago, Illinois

Dear Mr. Robert Kennedy,

It would be real keen if you could send me a picture of you, your wife and 9 kids.

The reason is I am a big Kennedy fan and I never had a picture before of a famous person with so many kids.

> Love,
> Sharon R
> Bronx, New York

Dear Mr. Kennedy,

I think it was terrific that you climbed the mountain because I would like to climb a mountain when I grow up.

So far the only thing I have ever climbed is a big rock in the backyard.

> Your friend,
> Andy W
> Tucson, Arizona

Dear Senator Kennedy,

Can I come to your house and play with your children?

I have no brothers or sisters. Only a cat.

I am very lonely.

> Love,
> Ross B
> Akron, Ohio

Dear Senator Kennedy,

I would like your opinion.

There is a water shortage in New York. Do you think I should take a bath every day?

> Your pal,
> Bruce R
> New York City, New York
> Age 9

Dear Senator Kennedy,

I am a 12 year old boy from Miami.

I read your book The Enemy Within and I liked it very much except that it had too many big words.

> Yours sincerely,
> Raymond R
> Miami, Florida

Dear Senator Kennedy,

President Kennedy was my best friend and I didn't even know him.

> Yours truly,
> Rachel G
> Salt Lake City, Utah

Dear Mr. Senator,

I would like to come to Washington and talk to you because I have a lot of troubles in my family and I know that you will understand and because you have had a lot of troubles in your family too.

If you say yes I would like to bring my husband with me because he is part of my troubles.

> Sincerely yours,
> Mrs. Jay L
> Chicago, Illinois

Dear Mr. Senator,

I have a friend. His name is Jerry Kennedy but I would like to get to know you because I only know Jerry and I don't know any real Kennedys.

Yours truly,
Jimmy K
Honesdale, Pennsylvania

Dear Senator Kennedy,

I heard on TV that you are a very good swimmer.

I am a good swimmer too but my mother makes me wear a life jacket.

She is a very nervous mother.

Sincerely,
Jayson R
Westport, Connecticut

Dear Senator Robert Kennedy,

I am writing this letter to wish you a happy birthday.

I don't know exactly when your birthday is but please read this letter wishing you a happy birthday from me on the exact day.

Yours truly,
Rex G
Buffalo, New York

Dear Senator Kennedy,

I think that you and your Ted should flip a coin to see who will run for President.

You take heads and he takes tails. If the coin comes up heads then you run for President.

It is the only fair way.

Sincerely yours,
Richard W
Long Beach, California

Dear Senator Kennedy,

It must really be something to have 9 kids.

You must have to pay a fortune in allowances every week.

Yours truly,
Mr. Harry G
Akron, Ohio

Dear Senator,

It would be the biggest thrill of my life if I could ever talk to you on the telephone.

Could you call me? I would call you but I can't afford long distance.

Sincerely,
Shirley R
Weston, Connecticut

Dear Senator Kennedy,

I like to listen to your speeches.

I think you are the best talker in Washington.

> Yours truly,
> Brad P
> Detroit, Michigan

Dear Robert Kennedy,

May I call you Bobby?

You see I am a 12 year old girl and I think I have a real big crush on you.

I hope that you aren't embarrassed. It's just that I think you are so cute. I know that it sounds funny to have a crush on a married man with nine children but thats the way it is.

I hope you won't laugh at this letter because I am very sincere.

If I ever got to meet you in person I would faint.

> Love,
> Anonymous
> Cleveland, Ohio

Dear Senator Kennedy,

I think Kennedy is the most famous name in America except for the Beatles.

> Love,
> Ida G
> Portland, Maine

Dear Robert Kennedy,

We would like to invite you to join our Robert Kennedy fan club.

It cost 50¢ to join our Robert Kennedy fan club but you can join for 15¢ because you are Robert Kennedy and we don't feel we should charge Robert Kennedy 50¢ to join the Robert Kennedy fan club.

> Your loyal fan,
> Amy L
> Club President
> Baltimore, Maryland

Dear Mr. Senator Kennedy,

I think it is terrific that you have 9 kids and you still smile.

> Yours truly,
> Angela S
> Washington, D. C.

Dear Robert Kennedy,

That day in November will go down in history as the blackest day in American history.

No American will ever forget it.

The name of John F. Kennedy will remain in our hearts as long as there is an American.

> Respectfully,
> Morris G
> Albany, New York

Dear Senator Kennedy,

If I ever got to meet you in person I wouldn't know what to say.

I would even be to nervous to say hi!

Yours truly,
Randy C
Riverdale, New York

Dear Senator Kennedy,

Someday the U.S.A. will have a lady President and I hope that the first lady President of the U.S.A. is Caroline Kennedy.

Yours truly,
William H
Jackson, Mississippi

Dear Senator Kennedy,

I am 9. I live in Detroit. Someday I bet I will be President of the U.S.A. and I haven't even got one vote yet.

Your friend,
Ted E
Detroit, Michigan

Dear Senator Kennedy,

Here are the things we need for New York City.
1) New schools
2) New roads
3) New parks
4) New houses
5) New baseball team.

Your citizen,
Larry G
New York City, New York

Dear Senator Kennedy,

I think it is terrific that you climb mountains and shoot the rapids.

We never did have a Senator like that before. Most Senators just sit and talk all the time.

Sincerely,
Harriet L
Syracuse, New York

Dear Senator Kennedy,

Which is your favorite book about Pres. Kennedy.

I only saved up $2 so I can only buy one good cheap book about him.

Your friend,
Irwin Z
Denver, Colorado

Dear Senator Kennedy,

I think you should be President of the U.S.A. in 1972. Please talk this over with President Johnson.

> Sincerely,
> May G
> Toledo, Ohio

Dear Bobby Kennedy,

There was a story in a magazine about you and in the story it said that sometimes you take your dog to the office with you.

You're lucky. I can't take my dog anywhere except to the grocery store.

> Your friend,
> Johnny G
> Hartford, Connecticut

Dear Senator Kennedy,

This letter is from Mickey. I am 8. I liked President Kennedy.

Did you know any other Presidents?
Did you know Lincoln and Washington?

> Love,
> Patricia M
> Raleigh, North Carolina

Dear Mr. Bobby Kennedy,

I think you are the best Senator and I don't even know what you do.

Love,
Merry L
Brooklyn, New York

Dear Senator Robert Kennedy,

I would like to change my name to Kennedy. I think it will help me in politics some day.

Your friend,
Humphrey B
Kansas City, Missouri

Dear Senator Kennedy,

I am for you. I think you are great.

Please remember this letter when you become President.

Your pal,
Rodger S
Brooklyn, New York

Dear Mr. Robert Kennedy,

I have seen you on TV and I think you are very hand-some.

You are almost as good looking as Dr. Kildare and you aren't even a real doctor.

> Love,
> Lilly C
> Boston, Massachusetts

Dear Senator Kennedy,

I believe that all America wants you for President and I haven't even talked to all of America. Just a few kids from my block.

> Your friend,
> Nelson G
> Toledo, Ohio

Dear Robert Kennedy,

I would like to ask you this question.

What is the hardest thing a Senator has to do? Is it to talk a lot?

> Very truly yours,
> Jerry G
> Chicago, Illinois

Dear R. Kennedy,

Our country will never be the same without John F Kennedy.

He was more than just a President. He was the kind of man that every American could look up to and admire. He was an inspiration to every American — young and old.

In my humble opinion he was one of the great Americans of the 20th century. You must have been very proud of your brother.

Sincerely,
Harry A
Spokane, Washington

Dear Senator Kennedy,

I would like to help you write your speeches.

I think I would be a big help because I know plenty of good words and lots of terrific jokes.

Sincerely,
Mitzi G
Richmond, Virginia

Dear Senator Kennedy,

Are you for or against taxes?

My father would like your opinion before the next election.

Sincerely,
Sandy S
Madison, Wisconsin

Dear Senator Kennedy,

I think John F Kennedy was our best President ever and not just because he liked touch football like me.

> Robert C
> Atlanta, Georgia

Dear Senator Robert Kennedy,

I don't believe that you should run for President of the U.S.A. because ex-Presidents never have anything to do.

> Your pal,
> Lloyd R
> Purchase, New York

Dear Senator Kennedy,

I believe that John F. Kennedy was the best looking President we ever had. He was even better looking than George Washington.

> Best wishes,
> Harriet G
> Fort Smith, Arkansas

Dear Robert Kennedy,

I remember President Kennedy in my prayers every night but last Saturday night because I was too tired to even say my prayers for anyone.

> Love,
> Joan G
> Chicago, Illinois

Dear Mr. Kennedy,

If there is any trouble with the Russians you should call our Boy Scout troop.

We have the best troop in Brooklyn and we are very strong and smart.

Our scout master is pretty good too.

Yours,
Jeffry G
Brooklyn, New York

Dear Senator Kennedy,

I have always been a big fan of yours even when you were just the President's kid brother.

Sincerely,
Mike M
Scranton, Pennsylvania

Dear Mr. Kennedy,

I like to read about President Kennedy but all the books are too hard for me.

Could you please write a book about President Kennedy with easy words for kids.

Thank you,
Bruce R
Oakland, California

Dear Senator Robert Kennedy,

I think you are doing a great job as a U. S. Senator and the thing I like best is you don't talk too much.

Best wishes,
Harry A
Spokane, Washington

Dear Senator Kennedy,

I hope you don't run for President until 1980.
That is when I will be 21 and I can vote for you.
I would like you to wait.

Sincerely,
Natalie L
Gainesville, Georgia

Dear Senator Robert Kennedy,

We can all hold our heads a little higher because John F. Kennedy was our President.
He made us all proud to be Americans.

Respectfully,
Wallace H
Larchmont, New York

P.S. I am writing this letter even though I am a 100% Republican.

Dear Mr. Robert Kennedy,

I think you are the best Senator we ever had for New York named Kennedy.

Your friend,
Marsha C
Syracuse, New York

Dear Mr. Robert Kennedy,

Me and my friend Arthur want to start a Robert Kennedy for President club.

Please send us $2 so we can make posters and buttons. We know we can help you a lot but we are broke.

Your friends,
Sidney and Arthur
Baton Rouge, Louisiana

Dear Mr. Kennedy,

I hope someday you are President of the U.S.A.

Love,
Gilda C
Philadelphia, Pennsylvania

P.S. Please don't tell Mr. Johnson I wrote this letter.

Dear Senator Robert Kennedy,

Please tell me which Kennedy I should root for to be President. Robert Kennedy or Ted Kennedy?

Yours truly,
Barry B
Staten Island, New York

Dear Senator Robert F. Kennedy,

I hope that you don't consider me disrespectful for writing this letter but it seems to me that since you became a United States Senator you have been very quiet. Shouldn't you speak out more on the important issues of the day?

You are the heir to the fine record your brother made as a Senator and as President and we all accept your leadership for these difficult times.

Respectfully,
Mrs. Lawrence G
Amarillo, Texas

Dear Senator Kennedy,

You are my idol. Imagine a grown woman of 35 who has an idol.

I even blush when I think about it.

The last time I had an idol was in 1950 and his name was Frank Sinatra.

Love,
Mrs. Mickey M
Marion, Ohio

Dear Senator Kennedy,

Can I come down to your office in Washington and discuss with you, Vietnam, the peace corp, the poverty program, medicare, federal aid to education, and housing.

I won't take up much of your time. All I need is five minutes.

Very truly,
Barbara G
Brookline, Massachusetts

Dear Senator Kennedy,

My husband was killed in an automobile accident a week after the tragic death of President Kennedy.

I was very depressed after my husband's death and I would not talk to anyone or go out in the street and I ate very little. My friends and relatives tried to cheer me up but it didn't work. I just wanted to die myself.

Then one day my little 12 year old nephew visited me and said "Aunt Stella, you should be brave. Look how Bobby Kennedy kept going after the assassination."

That is when I realized how wrong I was and how my husband would have wanted me to have courage.

Your determination and strength have been my inspiration and I am very grateful.

Sincerely,
Mrs. Barry M
Chicago, Illinois

Dear Bobby Kennedy,

I hope you don't mind me calling you Bobby.

The reason I call you Bobby is because you seem like one of the family.

I feel the same way about Teddy, Joan, Ethel and Jackie.

And of course our beloved Jack who will always be part of our family.

Yours truly,
Mrs. Marie K
Panama City, Florida

Dear Senator Kennedy,

I am not going to write a long letter because I know how busy you are.

The only thing I want in the whole world is your autograph.

I love all the Kennedys very much and I love to have all their autographs.

I don't care who it is as long as he or she's last name is Kennedy.

I even would like to have your new baby's autograph if he could write or make his X.

Love,
Bertha J
Hammond, Indiana

Dear Mr. Kennedy,

Please get rid of all the Communist people in U. S. A.

Your pal,
Peter M
Age 9
Salt Lake City, Utah

Dear Mr. Robert F. Kennedy,

My sister is a great fan of yours but she says she doesn't want to be thought of as a fan because fans are people who like the Beatles.

All she ever talks about is you and your family. I thought this would stop in a month but now 8 months later I give up.

On November 3 (election night) she was sent to bed before she found out whether you had won or not. So when my mother went to bed she got up and watched television until she found out. I found out when I heard her yell. Anything she ever does now has to do with you. Everyday she searches the newspaper to find articles about you.

I know there is nothing she would like better then a personal letter from you. Even if you just wrote "hello" and "goodbye".

Frankly a letter from you might keep her quiet for awhile. We are all a little tired of hearing about the Kennedys.

Sincerely,
Paula J
Greenville, South Carolina

Dear Senator,

In civics class I learned that since you are a Senator from New York I am one of your constituents (I hope I spelled it right).

I was very excited when I heard because I never was a constituent of a Kennedy before.

Yours truly,
Maurice D
Brooklyn, New York

Dear Senator Kennedy,

I would like a copy of the immigration law.
I want to get out of this city.

Sincerely,
Howard S
Chicago, Illinois

Dear Senator Kennedy,

For one year I have tried to purchase a realistic picture of President Kennedy to hang in my living room. I simply cannot find a good one.

I am in hopes that you will be able to supply me with information where I can obtain a truly life like picture.

I have only one picture hanging in my living room. It is a picture of Jesus Christ.

I have space for another picture—that of a beloved man, our President Kennedy.

Sincerely,
Isabel W
Swan Lake, New York

Dear Mr. Kennedy,

I was not happy when you became a Senator.

I had hoped that you would become Secretary of State or even Vice-President.

Your talents are too great to be wasted in the Senate. Senators may make a lot of noise but they don't get much done.

Let us hope that soon you will assume a greater position where you belong.

I have sent a copy of this letter to President Johnson.

> Truly yours,
> Roland W
> Kingsport, Tennessee

Dear Senator Kennedy,

Please let me have a picture of all your 9 kids with their names if you remember them all.

> Best regards,
> Carl L
> Stillwater, Oklahoma

Dear Senator Kennedy,

The people of New York gave the finest tribute to the memory of dear President Kennedy.

They elected you—United States Senator from New York.

> Yours sincerely,
> Mrs. Jayson L
> Rome, Pennsylvania

Dear Robert Kennedy,

My name is Linda and I am doing a science project on the science of handwriting and I was wondering if you would sign this card and write this sentence:

"Today is a fine day. Don't you think so."

If you did so this would greatly increase the value of my project.

I will be happy to send you an analysis of your handwriting free of charge.

Yours,
Linda M
Fairbanks, Alaska

Dear Robert Kennedy,

You and Mrs. Kennedy deserve a medal for courage. I hope you get one.

(Mrs.) Marion M
Hollywood, California

Dear Senator Kennedy,

Stop climbing mountains.

We need you in one piece for the future of our country.

Very truly,
Eugene M
Raleigh, North Carolina

Dear Senator Kennedy,

There are seven kids in my family and I am a twin. We admire your family very much.

I am all Irish only for one little bit that is Indian.

I know that JFK and RFK have done a lot for the Irish but I was wondering if you could tell me what you have done for the Indians.

Sincerely,
Jimmy K
Buffalo, New York

Dear Senator Kennedy,

All through the election I have worn your buttons that say Kennedy For Senator all over my shirt.

But that is not what I would like to talk to you about. You see, I am reading every book in our library at school that has something to do with space. This may sound funny but a Mickey Burke and I are trying to build a small spaceship about 2 ft. high.

We know what it is to be made of and how the engine works. Since you are a Senator we ask your help or suggestion.

In turn, if at any time for some reason you may need a plain boy like me, I will be at your service.

Your friend,
David K
Bronx, New York

Dear Senator Kennedy,

My husband and I are thinking about buying a farm. Could you please send us any government pamphlets you have on raising baby chicks, pigs, rabbits, sheep, cows, baby turkeys and on planting trees, corn, wheat and oats.

We would appreciate this information. We hope to be successful as farmers. We never were farmers before.

My husband and I are both Democrats and we voted for your brother so I think it is good that we will be farmers because the Democrats need more farm votes.

Yours very truly,
(Mrs.) Agnes J
Cleveland, Ohio

Dear Senator Kennedy,

I am writing this letter to you because we want a baseball field at Hunts Point.

I am writing to you because I know that you can do something about it real fast.

I told my friends about this letter and they said you only liked football and you didn't care about a baseball field.

Please answer if you care about baseball.

Your fan,
Johnny G
Lawrence, Long Island,
New York

Dear Bobby Kennedy,

I would like your opinion of the book Fail Safe and also a Merry Christmas.

> Love,
> Jennifer G
> Chicago, Illinois

Dear Mr. Senator Kennedy,

At lunch time at our school we go to Dog and Burger to buy lunch.

Then we go over to Dot's Dairy across the street. They kick us out because we bought lunch over at the Dog and Burger. They get jealous. Could you do something about it.

> Thank you a lot,
> Stanley G
> Syracuse, New York

Dear Mr. Kennedy,

We plan to visit Washington D. C. for a day or two.

Would you be kind enough to give me the name of a nice hotel near Union Station where we could stay that has cheap rates and clean sheets.

> Sincerely,
> (Mrs.) Janet R
> Albany, New York

Dear Senator Kennedy,

My sister and I will be visiting Washington to see all the sights and we would like to see you.

> Yours,
> Rita G
> Pittsburgh, Pennsylvania

Dear Mr. Kennedy,

We would like some information on the museums, art galleries and other public buildings in Washington. We need to know the places of interest to a group of 12 year old children.

Please include also parking facilities for a 20 foot trailer.

> Respectfully,
> Albert K
> Indianapolis, Indiana

Dear Senator Kennedy,

I like you very much. I wish you were the Senator from California.

No offense to the Senator from California but I don't even know his name and I do yours.

> Your fan,
> Diane P
> San Francisco, California

Dear Senator Robert Kennedy,

I am coming to Washington on Tuesday. Could you make sure Congress is in session.

Best wishes,
Morris B
Denver, Colorado

Dear Senator Kennedy,

I think in the next election you should run for President and your brother Ted should run for Vice-President.

Then we will be sure we have a Kennedy for President.

Regards,
Raymond M
Los Angeles, California

Dear Senator Kennedy,

I saw you on TV at the St. Patrick's Day parade and everybody was shaking your hand.

I want to know if you could give me a picture of you standing next to John F. Kennedy.

Yours truly,
Ruth K
New Haven, Connecticut

P.S. I'm sorry to have to mention John F. Kennedy in this letter.

Dear RFK,

I watched the Gemini space shot. It was very exciting. I got to thinking. Why don't they name a rocket after your brother President Kennedy?

Who names the rockets? Is he a Republican?

> A pal,
> Peter M
> Age 7½
> Denver, Colorado

Dear Senator Kennedy,

In my English class I am doing a term paper on your brother John.

I am finding him very interesting to do research on, however, I can only find information on him starting at 12 years old.

I was wondering if you had any spare time if you could tell me some things he did in his younger years.

If you don't remember too much maybe you could ask your mother or your brother Ted.

> Sincerely,
> Jay W
> Oakland, California

Dear Mr. Kennedy,

I would like your opinion as to whether Congress should be abolished.

> Robert B
> Birmingham, Alabama

Dear Senator,

What is more dangerous—Communism or smoking?

> Yours truly,
> Neil G
> Denver, Colorado

Dear Senator Kennedy,

I am doing a paper on the problems of democracy. Do we have any?

> Respectfully,
> Wallace G
> Boston, Massachusetts

Dear Robert Kennedy,

For some time now I have been trying to obtain a Kennedy Memorial Half Dollar.

They cannot be obtained for less than three times face value. It is a shame that this is the only way they can be obtained. I would be grateful if you would send me a Kennedy half dollar for the fifty cents I am sending you.

I loved President Kennedy very much and I want to save the half dollar for my children and grandchildren.

I will never spend it even if I am down to my last half dollar.

> Yours truly,
> Mrs. Randolph G
> Boston, Massachusetts

Dear Robert Kennedy,

My name is Andrew and I am 10 years old. Our parish only has 30 families and most are poor.

We have a nice church but we have a very big debt. Our priest drives 70 miles each time he comes. We would like to have him live here but we have to pay our debt before we build him a house.

We have a picnic every year to help us raise money.

Would you please send a gift, little or big, with your name on it for us to auction at our May picnic.

We think we would make a lot of money with a gift with your name.

The name Kennedy is magic here.

Sincerely,
Nashville, Tennessee

Dear Mr. Kennedy,

I am 18 years old and attend Central High School in Nashville Tennessee.

I am not a true and long admirer of yours but I am becoming one.

I am writing this letter because I want to urge you to run for the Presidency. In my opinion you represent the youth of today. In times past politicians were elder men. You and your family have changed that.

Now people respect the thoughts and words of young people because of you and your brother.

You and all the Kennedys have done a lot for all of us.

Respectfully,
Mitchell G
Akron, Ohio

Dear Mr. Kennedy,

How can I get some of the Poverty that everyone talks about?

Debbie G
Milwaukee, Wisconsin

Dear Mr. Kennedy,

In school we are studying about the first 13 colonies of the U. S. A.

Could you please send me the names of the Kennedys who were in the 13 colonies.

Your friend,
Alex J
Mobile, Alabama

Dear Senator Robert F. Kennedy,

The death of your brother hurt me deeply for he seemed to instill in me a feeling of gladness that I was alive and in America.

I am sure he would be proud to see the fine way you are carrying on his good work in the U. S. Senate.

You do the Kennedy name honor.

Sincerely,
Walter H
Fargo, North Dakota

Dear Senator Kennedy,

I am glad that you and your brother are in Washington because we have plenty of trouble there.

Yours sincerely,
Johnny G
New York City, New York

Dear Senator Kennedy,

The reason for this letter is to tell you what a wonderful woman I think your wife Ethel is. I have seen pictures and read about her since 1960 when I first heard about you.

I think she is the greatest woman in the world today.

I would like to see Ethel become the first lady because she is a great woman for all the women of America to look up to.

I believe that behind every great man there is a great woman.

Yours sincerely,
Mrs. Claudine J
Newark, New Jersey

Dear Senator,

You are very smart to have 9 kids.

Now when you run for President you already have nine more votes than the other feller.

Your fan,
Randy G
Pittsburgh, Pennsylvania

Dear Senator Kennedy,

I am in politics like you.

Last week I ran for president of my school and I won.

But I'll let you in on a little secret. I have forty first cousins who live nearby and they all go to my school. It sure helped when it came to the election.

I know that you helped your brother Jack get elected President and I hope that your brother Ted will help you get elected President in the next election.

One of the ways I got my relatives to vote for me was to tell them "Look what RFK did for JFK."

Yours truly,
Bruce L
Minneapolis, Minnesota

Dear Senator Kennedy,

I read in a newspaper that since that tragic day in November you have been spending a lot of time with Caroline and John Jr.

I know that you are very busy as a United States Senator but your devotion to your nephew and niece is one of the admirable qualities that we have come to expect from the Kennedys.

Sincerely,
Mrs. Alvin E
New York City, New York

Dear Senator Kennedy,

I sincerely hope you don't mind my saying this but you will need some practice if you are going to be as effective a speaker as your brother.

Your voice is okay but you don't seem to know what to do with your hands. Also your brother smiled more than you.

These are just helpful suggestions. I know what I am talking about because I am a pretty rotten speaker myself.

> Yours truly,
> Bart G
> Dayton, Ohio

Dear Senator Kennedy,

What are you doing to make sure that John F. Kennedy Jr. is President in 2005?

Plans should be made NOW!!

> Yours sincerely,
> Barbara G
> Malden, Massachusetts

Dear Senator Kennedy,

I am glad that when your brother was President he gave you a good job as Attorney General.

I hope that when you are President you will take good care of your brother, Ted.

> Sincerely,
> Louis W
> New Haven, Connecticut

Dear Senator,

As a negro I will always be grateful for what President Kennedy has done for the negro people.

Kennedy and Lincoln are the two Presidents we will honor forever.

I know that we can depend on you.

> Sincerely,
> Lawrence G
> Brooklyn, New York

Dear Mr. Robert Kennedy,

To be very frank with you I believe that your brother Ted is better looking than you are but don't despair. The good lookers don't always get the votes.

I'm for you.

> Love,
> Mitzi G
> Raleigh, North Carolina

Dear Mr. Kennedy,

First you were Attorney General, then you became a United States Senator. Next I think you should get to be Secretary of State and then in 1972 I think you should be the President.

Do you like my plan?

> Your friend,
> Walter J
> Chicago, Illinois

Dear Senator Kennedy,

When you climbed Mt. Kennedy in Canada I thought it was great and then when you shot the rapids in a canoe I thought it was sensational.

Please tell me what your next adventure will be.

> Best regards,
> Emile L
> Atlanta, Georgia

Dear Mr. Robert Kennedy,

The big problem you have is you look too young. Your wonderful brother looked young but you look younger.

Most people won't vote for somebody that looks like a kid for President even if his name is Kennedy.

May I suggest that you grow a mustache.

You may not like one but it sure will help to put you in the White House.

> Sincerely,
> Andrea B
> Westport, Connecticut

Dear Senator Kennedy,

You are the first Senator New York ever had with a Boston accent and I think it is great.

> Love,
> Mary Lou B
> Boston, New York

Dear Senator Kennedy,

It was very brave of you to climb Mt. Kennedy in honor of your brother but frankly I don't think that a man with 9 kids should take such a chance.

I have 8 kids and my wife won't even let me fly.

Sincerely,
Ralph W
Detroit, Michigan

Dear Senator Kennedy,

I know that you always have been a leader in the program for physical fitness and I was just wondering why you haven't gone on any 50 mile hikes lately.

Are you getting too old? If you don't set an example, our youth will grow up to be flabby men.

Yours truly,
Hilda G
Malden, Massachusetts

Dear Mr. Robert Kennedy,

You and Mrs. Jacqueline Kennedy and the entire Kennedy family were very brave at the funeral of our President.

I know how heavy your heart must have been and yet you acted like true soldiers.

Your actions were an inspiration to us all.

Sincerely,
Margaret G
Washington, D. C.

Dear Senator Kennedy,

How many pets do you have including your children?

Sincerely,
Ralph G
Warwick, Rhode Island

Dear Senator Robert Kennedy,

Many people expected you to be bitter and withdrawn after that unbelievable event that took the life of our President. If you had been bitter we would have understood.

Instead you have molded a brand new career for yourself as a United States Senator. And you are going to be a great Senator.

You have lived up to the very people your brother wrote about in his book Profiles In Courage. You are a brave young man.

Yours,
Beatrice G
Springfield, Illinois

Dear Mr. Robert Kennedy,

Please send me the story of your life. I am very interested.

Yours,
Mildred P
Dallas, Texas

P.S. Make sure you leave out the boring parts.

103

Dear Robert Kennedy,

I don't think it is fair that you are the Senator from New York and that your brother is the Senator from Massachusetts.

What are the people in the other 48 states supposed to do?

Sincerely,
Mrs. Murray G
Denver, Colorado

Dear Senator Kennedy,

Congratulations on your new baby. I read that this is your ninth child.

Is that a record for a U. S. Senator?

Yours truly,
Herbert D
St. Paul, Minnesota

Dear Senator Kennedy,

I understand that as a freshman Senator you are not supposed to talk too much. That is an unwritten rule of the U. S. Senate.

But I feel that you should be the exception to the rule. Every citizen is looking to you for words of guidance. Please speak out, Mr. Kennedy, on the vital issues that affect us all. Your voice is a comfort to us all.

Respectfully,
Lee J
Chicago, Illinois

Dear Senator Kennedy,

    I like you.

    I like Ted Kennedy.

    I like Mrs. Jackie Kennedy and I like all the other Kennedys too but I don't know their exact name.

> Your pal,
> Norman B
> Syracuse, New York

Dear Mr. Kennedy,

    Please send me a lock of your hair for my scrapbook.

    You have plenty of hair so I know you can spare a little for me.

> Love,
> Jennifer S
> Pittsburgh, Pennsylvania

Dear Senator Kennedy,

    I know that your slogan when you were running for U. S. Senator was "Let's Put Bobby Kennedy to work for New York."

    I hope and pray that the day will not be too distant when I will hear the slogan—"Let's Put Bobby Kennedy to Work for the U.S.A."

> Yours very truly,
> Mrs. Nelson G
> Walla Walla, Washington

Dear Senator Kennedy,

I am one of your constituents and a staunch supporter of the liberal wing of the Democratic party.

I am a student of government and I am now investigating the hypothesis of a military takeover of the United States Government by the military as presented in Seven Days In May and Fail Safe.

Do you think this is possible? If so, do you think it would be a wise move for a young man like me to join the armed forces so I can be on the winning side when that day comes.

Yours,
Anthony P
Alexandria, Virginia

Dear Senator Kennedy,

One of the most important problems facing America and the world today is the population explosion.

The world is getting too crowded and there isn't food to go around.

I firmly believe that the great leaders of our country like you must set an example so that we can stop this population explosion.

I know that it is none of my business Senator but 9 kids doesn't help to inspire other people.

Yours respectfully,
Lorraine R
New York City, New York

Dear Senator Kennedy,

Could you please send me a picture of yourself. Preferably one of your profile which I think looks better than your full face.

A loyal Kennedy fan,
Ruth D
Bronx, New York

Dear Mr. Senator,

I know that you can do anything!
Please. Please get some rain for New York.
We need lots! Right away!

Arnie K
Queens, New York

Dear Senator Kennedy,

I have two tickets to Congress for June 18.
Please make sure something is going on. Not just a lot of talk.

Murphy K
Indianapolis, Indiana

Dear Senator Kennedy,

I believe that you would have been elected Senator even if your name wasn't Kennedy but I guess it didn't hurt.

Best wishes,
Milton E
Housedale, Pennsylvania

Dear Mr. Robert Kennedy,

I heard that you are very shy.

I am shy too. Someday I hope to be a U. S. Senator like you.

That will give the U.S.A. *two* shy Senators.

> Yours,
> Jay W
> Lansing, Michigan

Dear Senator,

I have been an admirer of the Kennedy family for some time and would be extremely pleased if you could send me the following item:

1) One set of instructions and rules of touch football.

> Many thanks,
> Ronnie M
> Pueblo, Colorado

Dear Robert Kennedy,

I am a widow and a great admirer of President Kennedy.

I saw a picture of your Christmas card.

I would like to get your Christmas card next Christmas. It would mean a lot to me. Since my husband died the only Christmas card I get is from the bank.

> Very sincerely,
> Mrs. Homer G
> Huntsville, Alabama

Dear Senator Robert F. Kennedy,

I am very proud of the fact that I have had the opportunity to vote for two Kennedys.

First I voted for your brother for President and now I have voted for you for Senator.

I only wish I could live in New York and Boston so I could have voted for Ted for Senator too!

I have dedicated my life to voting for Kennedys forever and ever.

> Yours truly,
> Mrs. Helen M
> Buffalo, New York

Dear Senator Robert F. Kennedy,

I know that you are a good Democrat but don't you think you could give some help to the Republicans.

They are in big trouble.

> Yours truly,
> Angela S
> Los Alamos, New Mexico

Dear Senator Kennedy,

An assassin's bullet can take his life but it can never take the spirit and memory of John F. Kennedy from us.

We are fortunate to have a man like you who will keep his good work and shining example alive forever.

> Sincerely,
> Mrs. Harriet G
> Providence, Rhode Island

Dear Senator,

I would appreciate it if you would send me a summary of U. S. foreign policy since the war of 1812.

I need it for a term paper and the summary can't be more than one page long.

Sincerely,
Charlie H
New London, Connecticut

Dear Senator Kennedy,

I have a great idea for kids 8 years old to kids 14 years old.

It's like this. We kids should have little industries so we could make our own buildings, houses and stores, sell cars exactly like grown up cars except kid size.

We could have our own employees like the grownups do except we work alone.

And even our own President of the states for us kids (a kid President of course).

We could have our own freeways, highways, avenues and our own little citys and towns.

If we could have all of this Mr. Kennedy by the time we grow up we could advance the states 20 years ahead.

I know that you will like this idea because you are in favor of kids.

Your pal,
Mickey K
Battle Creek, Michigan

Dear Robert Kennedy,

Congratulations for your new son Matthew.

I saw him the day he was baptized. He's cute.

I was right next to your car and if you remember someone saying to you that "I belong to a family of 13 going on 14". Well that was me.

Don't you just love big families!

> Yours truly,
> Alma R
> Miami, Florida

Dear Mr. Kennedy,

I never get tired reading about the Kennedy family.

Some days I can read about you for 15 minutes without stopping.

> Mickey J
> Age 10
> Key West, Florida

Dear Senator Robert F. Kennedy,

A friend of mine told me something and I would like to know if it is true.

Does a Senator have to be a good actor?

> Very truly,
> Scott M
> New York City, New York

Dear Senator Robert Kennedy,

I know that many people object to your climbing mountains and shooting rapids but in my opinion you should do more of it.

Our nation needs more men of action and spirit like you.

We have too many leaders who just sit around and do nothing but talk.

I like people with get up and go.

> Best regards,
> Angela S
> Altoona, Pennsylvania

Dear Senator Bobby Kennedy,

Please let me have a map of Fort Knox.

> Jay R
> Hartford, Connecticut

Dear Senator Kennedy,

How is your family and you?

My mother got your picture and we thank you very much for sending it. But we had an accident. My brother was so excited he tore the envelope and the picture.

Could you please send us another picture in a stronger envelope.

> Irving G
> Rye, New York

Dear Robert Kennedy,

Send me information on teenage marriages.
I am 12 and I will be ready soon.

Yours truly,
Hilda K
Cincinnati, Ohio

Dear Senator Kennedy,

I know that it is difficult for you to step into your
brother's shoes but all America is counting on you to
carry on.

The memory of your brother must be very painful but
I hope and pray that you will find the courage to go forward with his dream of a better America.

Sincerely yours,
Miss Helen H
Beverly Hills, California

Dear Senator Kennedy,

I would like very much to come and live at your house
for a day.

I never lived in a Senator's house before and I would
like to start with you.

Please send me your address. I won't be much trouble
and I will help dry the dishes and throw out the gar-
bage.

Your fan,
Ralph G
Cleveland, Ohio

Dear Senator Kennedy,

Whenever I feel sad and blue about what happened to President Kennedy, I think about you and I feel much better. I know that you will keep his memory alive with your good work.

Very sincerely,
Harry S
Providence, Rhode Island

Dear Bobby Kennedy,

I feel I can call you Bobby because I have read so much about you and I feel I can call your brother Teddy because I have read so much about him.

I read a lot about President Kennedy too but I always called him Mr. President because he was the President and to call him Jack wouldn't be respectful.

Yours,
Louis G
New York City, New York

Dear Senator Kennedy,

When President Kennedy left us I felt as though I had lost a son. Every mother felt that way.

He was every mother's ideal son. Strong, handsome, brilliant and fine. Now that he is gone it is every mother's duty to see to it that their sons follow his example.

Respectfully,
Mrs. Gloria G
Kingsport, Tennessee

Dear Mr. Kennedy,

I read in a magazine that you and your brother Ted are the first set of brothers in the U.S. Senate since 1803.

I think that it is wonderful. Someday my children and their children will read how the Kennedys made history again.

> Your fan,
> (Mrs.) Jack H
> Cleveland, Ohio

Dear Senator Kennedy,

Your brother President Kennedy did a lot of good things for the young people.

I hope you will carry on his good work and do something for the young people and the people who aren't so young anymore like me. I am 15.

> Yours truly,
> Jennifer L
> Canton, Ohio

Dear Senator Kennedy,

May I please have permission to interview you for my school paper.

300 people read my school paper and that's a lot of votes some day.

> Sincerely yours,
> Hillard W
> Editor
> Bayonne, New Jersey

Dear Senator Kennedy,

The thing that I admired most about President Kennedy were his great speeches especially his inauguration speech.

I still like to read his speeches and when I do sometimes I feel very sad. He had such a beautiful command of the english language.

John F. Kennedy may have left us but his magnificent words will live forever.

> Sincerely,
> Mr. Jerry C
> Bayone, New York
> Bayonne, New Jersey

Dear Senator Robert Kennedy,

All the kids in our class voted you our favorite U. S. Senator.

I think you won because everybody liked you and nobody knew the name of any other Senator.

> Yours,
> Anzela W
> Harrisburg, Pennsylvania

Dear Senator Robert F Kennedy,

I am sending you one of my rabbit's feet. It will bring you plenty of good luck.

Please send me back 25¢ for the rabbit's foot. It will be worth it. Good luck is worth plenty more than 25¢.

> Yours,
> Hillary G
> Anderson, Indiana

Dear Senator Kennedy,

Please mail to me the high points of your next speech as I haven't got time to read the whole thing.

Respectfully,
Paul H
Spokane, Washington

Dear Senator Bobby Kennedy,

You sure got a mess of kids.

We have 5 kids in our family and my mother says that's enough!

Your fan,
Joan G
Philadelphia, Pennsylvania

Dear Senator Kennedy,

I am a 13 year old boy. During the last campaign I put in hours passing out your pamphlets in Ithaca and talking to people about you.

Then you came to Ithaca and I was there at your rally in the park. I was in the front row and as you began to shake hands all of us reached for your hand. The person on my left shook hands with you but you didn't shake with me.

On Thursday I will be in Washington with my mother. Would it be possible for me to shake hands with you in your office since I missed last time?

Your friend,
Kwit Z
Ithaca, New York

Dear Senator Kennedy,

An assassin's bullet could take his life but never his memory in the hearts and minds of us all.

Yours truly,
Alan S
Greensboro, North Carolina

Dear Senator Kennedy,

Please write me a letter because I never got a letter from anybody important except my Uncle Arnold who is the firechief in Watertown.

Yours truly,
Andy W
Buffalo, New York

Dear Senator Kennedy,

I'll bet after 9 children you are running out of names.
Here are some names you can use for your future children.

Boys	Girls
Rex	Hilda
Milton	Tillie
Godfrey	Mellisa
Homer	Mildred
Stanton	Roberta
	Jennifer

If you need more names let me know but these should hold you for awhile.

Very truly,
Gloria G
Trenton, New Jersey

Dear Senator Kennedy,

I wish you would come and play football for the New York Graves.

We need a good quarterback.

> Yours truly,
> Howard G
> New York City, New York

Dear Senator Kennedy,

I am 8.
I visited President Kennedy's grave.
I was very sad.

> Louis P
> Indianapolis, Indiana

Dear Senator Robert Kennedy,

Do you spank your children when they are bad?
If the answer is no please answer this letter.
If the answer is yes don't bother to answer this letter.

> Your friends,
> Randy and Jeffry

Dear Senator Robert Kennedy,

I would like to join the Peace Corps before my final exam next week.

> Thank you,
> Patrick K
> Kansas City, Kansas

Dear Senator Kennedy,

I don't think it's right that all the Kennedys are Democrats.

It isn't fair to the Republicans. They never get to vote for a Kennedy.

Yours truly,
Andrew A
Westport, Connecticut

Dear Senator Kennedy,

I am the President of my class in school. I won the election over Herbie Waters because I gave all the kids in my class bubble gum on election day.

Why don't you give out bubble gum on next election day. Then nobody will be able to beat you.

Yours sincerely,
Jerry K
Honesdale, Pennsylvania

Dear Senator Kennedy,

One of the reasons I like you is you aren't afraid of anything.

You aren't afraid to climb mountains or go in a canal in dangerous water.

A lot of the other Senators are okay but they are afraid to climb mountains.

Your friend,
Katie G
Madison, Wisconsin